Newts

CW00864656

CONTENTS

Introduction

Newts are **amphibians.** They live on land as well as in water.

Great Crested newt

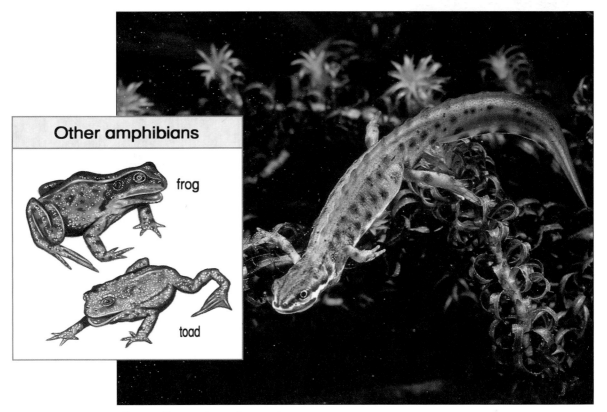

Other amphibians

frog

toad

Smooth newt under water

Newts have long tails and short legs.

A newt's tail is as long
as your little finger.

Newts on land

Newts are nocturnal.
They hunt for food at night.

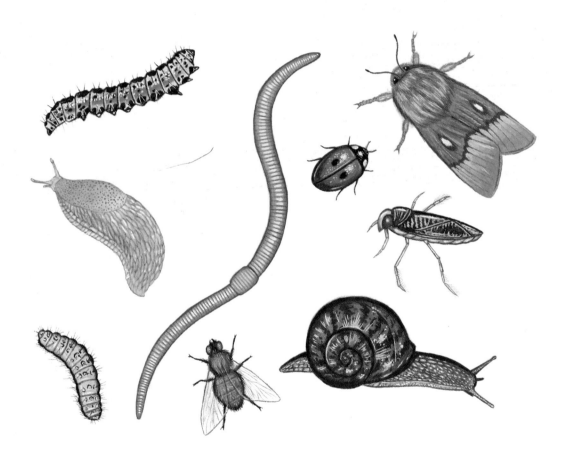

They eat worms, snails, slugs and insects.

Newts often hide in damp places.

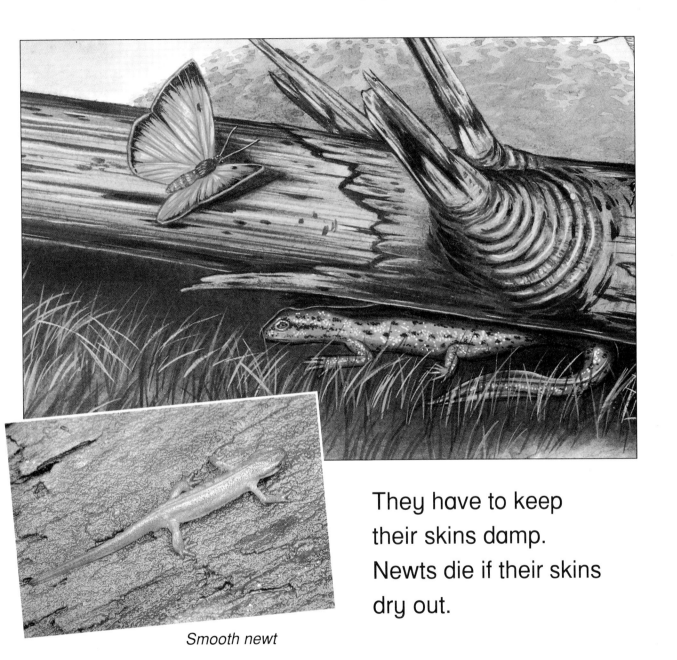

Smooth newt

They have to keep
their skins damp.
Newts die if their skins
dry out.

In the winter, most newts hibernate.

They hide away and go
into a deep sleep.

They do not move
or eat.

In the spring, newts look for water.
They often go to the same pond each year.

Newts in the water

Newts have a thick skin on land.
They need a different skin in the water.

Great
Crested
newt

They shed their skin when they go into the water.
The new skin is thin.

Newts shed their skin in one piece. They use their feet to peel the skin off their body. They often eat the old skin.

Smooth newt

Newts swim well. They can use their legs and their long flat tails.

In the water, male newts look for female newts.
Some male newts change colour.
Their bellies turn bright orange.

Great Crested newt

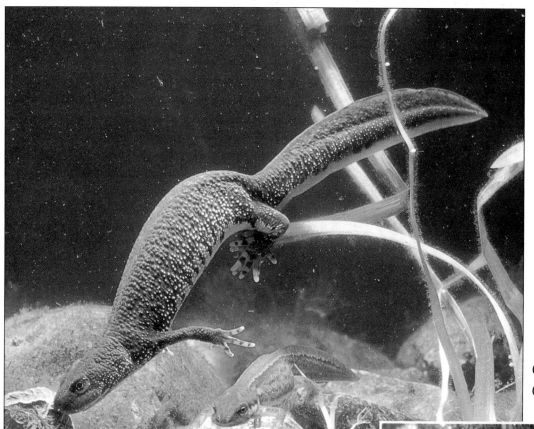

*Great
Crested newt*

The female newt lays lots of eggs.
She lays one egg at a time and
sticks it to a leaf. She uses her
feet to fold the leaf over.
The leaf hides the egg.

egg

How newts grow

The eggs hatch into tadpoles.
The tadpoles have long tails.

Tadpole in egg

They can soon swim well.
They eat tiny pond animals.

The tadpoles grow legs as they get bigger.

gills

Great Crested newt tadpole

Great Crested newt

The front legs grow first, then the back legs.
The tadpoles begin to look like newts.

This is how a newt grows.

Index